Nanaimo Girl

Nanaimo Girl

A Memoir by

Prudence Emery

Cormorant Books

The publisher gratefully acknowledges the support of the Canada Council for the Arts and the Ontario Arts Council for its publishing program. We acknowledge the financial support of the Government of Canada through the Canada Book Fund (CBF) for our publishing activities, and the Government of Ontario through Ontario Creates, an agency of the Ontario Ministry of Culture, and the Ontario Book Publishing Tax Credit Program.

LIBRARY AND ARCHIVES CANADA CATALOGUING IN PUBLICATION

Title: Nanaimo girl : a memoir / by Prudence Emery.
Names: Emery, Prudence, 1936– author.
Identifiers: Canadiana (print) 20200159143 | Canadiana (ebook) 20200159151 |
ISBN 9781770865273 (softcover) | ISBN 9781770865280 (HTML)
Subjects: LCSH: Emery, Prudence, 1936– | LCSH: Motion picture industry—Public relations. |
LCSH: Public relations personnel—Biography. | LCSH: Press agents—Biography. |
LCSH: Nanaimo (B.C.)— Biography. | LCGFT: Autobiographies.
Classification: LCC PN1998.3.E44 A3 2020 | DDC 659.2/979143092—dc23

Cover photo: Cover photo courtesy of Tomas Jaski Ltd.
Cover design: Angel Guerra / Archetype
Interior text design: tannicegdesigns.ca
Printer: Friesens

Printed and bound in Canada.

CORMORANT BOOKS INC.
260 SPADINA AVENUE, SUITE 502, TORONTO, ON M5T 2E4
www.cormorantbooks.com

To Krystyne and Scott Griffin,
who enhanced my life.

Contents

⸎

Nanaimo Girl

Centre of the Universe
1936 to 1957

&

Nanaimo! Nanaimo!

You get old and you realize there are no answers, just stories.
— GARRISON KEILLOR

DAD WAS HUFFING AND puffing as he hiked to Mount Benson west of Nanaimo — an anxious father-to-be — while Mum was huffing and puffing in the Nanaimo General Hospital — giving birth to me. The date was August 27, 1936. My birth increased the population of the town from 6,500 to 6,501.

My first real memory begins with me in a highchair. My parents were entertaining guests, all of whom were laughing uproariously. Through the din I was heard to say my first sentence and what was to become my mantra: "Isn't it funny!"

And it was funny, how I grew up in what was once a murky little coal town on lower Vancouver Island and behaved so badly that I was sent to a proper private school in Vancouver to learn my manners.

But Nanaimo is where I started. No big coal town, by 1936 it was moving into lumber, but for at least a hundred years, Nanaimo had been coal. In fact, one mine alone — and there were about fifty-seven — produced eighteen million tons of coal in total by 1937, the year that it closed, a year after I was born. By 1968, all the mines were finally closed.

The town was originally a handy little trading post on the inland side of the island. Then, in the mid-1800s, coal was discovered. The Hudson's Bay Company built a fort there in 1853, known as the Nanaimo Bastion. My junior high school featured a replica of the bastion, by then a symbol of the town. In 1887, Nanaimo experienced a blast in a mine caused by methane-infused coal dust that ignited. It was disastrous, and stood as the largest man-made explosion in Canadian history until the Halifax Explosion of 1917.

By the time I was in high school, Nanaimo had also come to be renowned for its many beer parlours. And since 1967, its annual highlight has been the Great International World Championship Bathtub Race.

I used to think that Nanaimo was the centre of the universe, and then I didn't. In fact, in a lifetime of rubbing shoulders with the rich and famous, almost no one I met had heard of Nanaimo, and they certainly didn't know how to pronounce it. So I became the girl from Nanaimo (wherever that was). And some eventually learned how to pronounce it: *Nah-nigh-moe.*

Nanaimo, although the coal was dwindling, still was rife with legend. Story has it that when white men arrived in boats in 1791, the natives ran up and down the beach shouting, "Nanaimo! Nanaimo!" ("*Snuneymuxw! Snuneymuxw!*") The greeting was taken as "Welcome! Welcome!" But it was probably more like "Bugger off! Bugger off!" The newcomers may not have buggered off, but I eventually did, for a series of adventures that were often anything but prudent. But I had to try to grow up first, and Nanaimo happened to be the place.

How my parents got there, that's another curiosity. They travelled between England and Canada before settling out west. Somehow, Dad managed to begin his ophthalmology practice in Nanaimo a mere two months after they arrived and a month before I was born.

They were both from the prairies. My father, Edward Douglas Emery, was born in Edmonton, Alberta, on May 12, 1897, third son of a prominent lawyer. The Emerys had emigrated from Norfolk in 1840, settling outside London in Upper Canada.

My mother, Lorna Doone Saville, was born in Spy Hill, Saskatchewan, on October 24, 1910, fourth of eleven children. The Savilles went back and forth from Saskatchewan to Suffolk, England, farming in both places, until they finally decided on ranching and bought an eight-thousand-acre spread in the Battle River Valley in east-central Alberta.

My parents met in 1933. Dad was en route to Vienna to complete his studies in eye, ear, nose, and throat surgery. "You've got to meet the Saville girls," insisted Dr. McPhail, his host in Hardisty, Alberta, ten miles from the Saville ranch. So he did.

On his first visit to the ranch, he was attempting to play the piano when someone said, "Puggy, let someone play who can play." Whereupon Mum hit the ivories with her usual style and captivated his heart. (Occasionally pugnacious, Dad was nicknamed Puggy).

Dad was smitten and, for the rest of his visit, courted Mum at the ranch, where her five brothers put the city slicker to the test. When they went riding, they loosened the girth on his saddle or rigged Dad's stirrups to fall off. Fortunately, Dad didn't fall off. After he returned to Europe, he proposed to Mum via long-distance telephone from Birmingham Eye Hospital, where he was house surgeon. They were married in Bradford, Yorkshire, on April 4, 1934, and for a year lived in Stoke-on-Trent while Dad commuted to Birmingham.

My parents returned to Canada in early 1936 and drove to Vancouver in a new Ford with a rumble seat. Mum was already pregnant with me. Dad completed his internship at Vancouver General Hospital before he and Mum moved to Nanaimo on Vancouver Island on July 1, 1936. When they arrived, they were two. Then they were three: I was born nearly two months later.

Growing Up in Nanaimo

IT MIGHT HAVE BEEN the middle of the Depression, but to me, childhood in Nanaimo was a carefree adventure.

Around age four, my personality had begun to emerge, and I was starting to take part in the sort of antics that would come to be typical of Nanaimo Girl. A favourite game was the Three Bears, which I played with Kibben and his younger brother, David, the sons of family friend Dr. Seriol Williams. Kibben was the daddy bear, I was the mummy bear, and David was the baby bear. But our parents didn't know about the other game we played: "I'll show you mine if you show me yours."

As I grew older, I was influenced by Auntie Dodie, who was an artist. I was always drawing. Dodie recalls that once we visited another family in Nanaimo, the Cunliffes. Mum had brought some drawing materials in her purse. Although I was looking angelic in a blue velvet dress with a lace collar, I drew a scathing cartoon in which Mrs. Cunliffe was dragging her husband by the ear. "It actually looked like them," laughed Dodie years later.

Once I sprayed Nanny (my father's mother) with the garden hose. My mum was in the house and spotted me watering Nanny and dashed out to stop the deluge. Mum and Dodie were shocked. But I just didn't like the prim and proper Victorian old lady.

I don't think Dad liked Nanny much either. This was verified many years later when my cousin John asked Dad why his father had died so young. "If you were married to my mother you might drink yourself to death too," my dad replied.

WHEN YOU'RE GROWING UP, you don't have a sense of what you'll look back on one day, decades in the future. Moments might seem part of your day-to-day life, coming and going, but when you're in your eighties, sitting back in a recliner, they re-emerge as flashes. Fond memories of my girlhood include the first time I managed to tie my own shoelaces and dressing up in outfits from my parents' costume box in the den. Then there was skating on the snow-packed streets of Nanaimo or on the dykes outside town, and bailing out my father's dinghy. (The dinghy was called *Bunpug*, an amalgam of his and his older brother's nicknames.)